# The Climate Emergency Journal

John Pabon

Copyright © 2021 John Pabon All rights reserved.

No part of this publication may be reproduced, distributed, or transmitted in any form or by any means, including photocopying, recording, or other electronic or mechanical methods, without the prior written permission of the publisher, except in the case of brief quotations embodied in reviews and certain other non-commercial uses permitted by copyright law.

John Pabon takes no responsibility for rising sea levels, increasing temperatures, strange weather patterns, or other incidences of global warming, calamity, or a dystopian future.

To learn more, go to johnpabon.com.

ISBN (print): 978-0-6489184-4-8

## Hello there!

You hold in your hands the key to saving our collective future and bringing us all back from the edge of extinction. No, it's not some miracle invention to clean the air. It's definitely not a check to fund your favorite charity. Nor is it the keys to an underground bunker somewhere in Scandinavia.

It's better than all of those. It's a plan.

As the saying goes, if you don't know where you're headed then any road will get you there. That's kind of how we've been trying to save the planet: lots of great ideas but no concerted strategy. Well, it's time to change all that!

Instead of getting angry, or cowering in fear, put pen to paper and get to work. Set goals every day, remind yourself of those critical wins, and even jot down what inspires you.

By the end, you'll be surprised how much a plan can light a fire under your butt to take action.

"I've starred in a lot of science fiction movies and, let me tell you something, climate change is not science fiction. This is a battle in the real world. It is impacting us right now."

Arnold Schwarzenegger

# How will you change the world today?

## What good happened today?

## Who or what is inspiring you?

"The Earth is a fine place and worth fighting for."

Ernest Hemingway

# How will you change the world today?

## What good happened today?

## Who or what is inspiring you?

"We do not inherit the Earth from our ancestors. We borrow it from our children."

Native American Proverb

# How will you change the world today?

## What good happened today?

## Who or what is inspiring you?

"We are running the most dangerous experiment in history right now, which is to see how much carbon dioxide the atmosphere can handle before there is an environmental catastrophe."

Elon Musk

# How will you change the world today?

## What good happened today?

## Who or what is inspiring you?

"It's not climate change that needs to be tackled. It is the political power of the fossil fuel industry."

Richard Denniss

# How will you change the world today?

## What good happened today?

## Who or what is inspiring you?

"One can see from space how the human race has changed the Earth. All of this is evidence that human exploitation of the planet is reaching a critical limit. We cannot continue to pollute the atmosphere, poison the ocean and exhaust the land. There isn't any more available."

Stephen Hawking

# How will you change the world today?

## What good happened today?

## Who or what is inspiring you?

"Twenty-five years ago people could be excused for not knowing much, or doing much, about climate change. Today we have no excuse."

Desmond Tutu

## How will you change the world today?

## What good happened today?

## Who or what is inspiring you?

"Climate change is the single greatest threat to a sustainable future but, at the same time, addressing the climate challenge presents a golden opportunity to promote prosperity, security and a brighter future for all."

Ban Ki-Moon

# How will you change the world today?

## What good happened today?

## Who or what is inspiring you?

"Let's double down on solar energy, let's be more energy-efficient, let's weatherize our homes. We can build a better, healthier economy based on good-paying, clean energy jobs."

Ian Somerhalder

# How will you change the world today?

## What good happened today?

## Who or what is inspiring you?

"We don't have time to sit on our hands as our planet burns. For young people, climate change is bigger than election or re-election. It's life or death."

Alexandria Ocasio-Cortez

# How will you change the world today?

## What good happened today?

## Who or what is inspiring you?

"The time for seeking global solutions is running out. We can find suitable solutions only if we act together and in agreement."

Pope Francis

# How will you change the world today?

## What good happened today?

## Who or what is inspiring you?

"Pollution and climate change by excessive burning of fossil fuels are real threats, not the people who warn that we must take these threats seriously."

David Suzuki

# How will you change the world today?

## What good happened today?

## Who or what is inspiring you?

"We really need to kick the carbon habit and stop making our energy from burning things. Climate change is also really important. You can wreck one rainforest then move, drain one area of resources and move onto another, but climate change is global."

Sir David Attenborough

# How will you change the world today?

## What good happened today?

## Who or what is inspiring you?

"The Earth is in a death spiral. It will take radical action to save us."

George Monbiot

# How will you change the world today?

## What good happened today?

## Who or what is inspiring you?

"Climate change is a terrible problem, and it absolutely needs to be solved. It deserves to be a huge priority."

Bill Gates

# How will you change the world today?

## What good happened today?

## Who or what is inspiring you?

"Climate change is a huge challenge, but it can be brought in line if governments, businesses and individuals work together."

Sir Richard Branson

# How will you change the world today?

## What good happened today?

## Who or what is inspiring you?

"It's not that the world hasn't had more carbon dioxide. It's not that the world hasn't been warmer. The problem is the speed at which things are changing. We are inducing a sixth mass extinction event kind of by accident and we don't want to be the 'extinctee.'"

Bill Nye

# How will you change the world today?

## What good happened today?

## Who or what is inspiring you?

"What you do makes a difference, and you have to decide what kind of difference you want to make."

Dr. Jane Goodall

# How will you change the world today?

## What good happened today?

## Who or what is inspiring you?

"The world is reaching the tipping point beyond which climate change may become irreversible. If this happens, we risk denying present and future generations the right to a healthy and sustainable planet — the whole of humanity stands to lose."

Kofi Annan

# How will you change the world today?

## What good happened today?

## Who or what is inspiring you?

"Climate change is real. It is happening right now, it is the most urgent threat facing our entire species and we need to work collectively together and stop procrastinating."

Leonardo Di Caprio

# How will you change the world today?

## What good happened today?

## Who or what is inspiring you?

"One thing leads to the other. Deforestation leads to climate change, which leads to ecosystem losses, which negatively impacts our livelihoods — it's a vicious cycle."

Gisele Bundchen

## How will you change the world today?

## What good happened today?

## Who or what is inspiring you?

"By polluting the oceans, not mitigating CO2 emissions and destroying our biodiversity, we are killing our planet. Let us face it, there is no planet B."

Emmanuel Macron

# How will you change the world today?

## What good happened today?

## Who or what is inspiring you?

"It's important for me to have hope because that's my job as a parent, to have hope, for my kids, that we're not going to leave them in a world that's in shambles, that's a chaotic place, that's a dangerous place."

James Cameron

# How will you change the world today?

## What good happened today?

## Who or what is inspiring you?

"We are the first generation to feel the effect of climate change and the last generation who can do something about it."

Barack Obama

# How will you change the world today?

## What good happened today?

## Who or what is inspiring you?

"I hope to use my celebrity to motivate people and contribute to moving our global society back from the brink. I am surprised environment is not at the top of the agenda. What is more important than good and clean air?"

Don Cheadle

## How will you change the world today?

## What good happened today?

## Who or what is inspiring you?

"Believe in the power of your own voice. The more noise you make, the more accountability you demand from your leaders, the more our world will change for the better."

Al Gore

# How will you change the world today?

## What good happened today?

## Who or what is inspiring you?

"Climate change is the greatest threat to our existence in our short history on this planet. Nobody's going to buy their way out of its effects."

Mark Ruffalo

# How will you change the world today?

## What good happened today?

## Who or what is inspiring you?

"I hold a vision of this blue green planet, safe and in balance. At the end of the Fossil Fuel Era, we are emerging to a new reality. We are ready to make the next leap — as momentous as abolishing slavery or giving women the vote."

Elizabeth May

## How will you change the world today?

## What good happened today?

## Who or what is inspiring you?

"Climate change knows no borders. It will not stop before the Pacific Islands and the whole of the international community here has to shoulder a responsibility to bring about sustainable development."

Angela Merkel

# How will you change the world today?

## What good happened today?

## Who or what is inspiring you?

"If you really think that the environment is less important than the economy, try holding your breath while you count your money."

Guy McPherson

# How will you change the world today?

## What good happened today?

## Who or what is inspiring you?

"Climate change is sometimes misunderstood as being about changes in the weather. In reality, it is about changes in our very way of life."

Paul Polman

# How will you change the world today?

## What good happened today?

## Who or what is inspiring you?

"I want you to act as if the house is on fire, because it is."

Greta Thunberg

# How will you change the world today?

## What good happened today?

## Who or what is inspiring you?

"We can't take climate change and put it on the back burner. If we don't address climate change, we won't be around as humans."

Conrad Anker

# How will you change the world today?

## What good happened today?

## Who or what is inspiring you?

"The world will not be destroyed by those who do evil, but by those who watch them without doing anything."

Albert Einstein

## How will you change the world today?

# What good happened today?

# Who or what is inspiring you?

"While the problem can sometimes seem overwhelming, we can turn things around — but we must move beyond climate talk to climate action."

Ted Turner

# How will you change the world today?

## What good happened today?

## Who or what is inspiring you?

"Men argue. Nature acts."

Voltaire

# How will you change the world today?

## What good happened today?

## Who or what is inspiring you?

"The future will be green or not at all."

Jonathon Porritt

# How will you change the world today?

## What good happened today?

## Who or what is inspiring you?

"I'm often asked whether I believe in global warming. I now just reply with the question: Do you believe in gravity?"

Neil deGrasse Tyson

# How will you change the world today?

## What good happened today?

## Who or what is inspiring you?

"Climate change isn't something in the future. That narrative is fundamentally flawed because there are millions impacted and so many displaced already. That is the new inconvenient truth that no one wants to hear."

Aneesa Khan

# How will you change the world today?

## What good happened today?

## Who or what is inspiring you?

"A nation that destroys its soils destroys itself. Forests are the lungs of our land, purifying the air and giving fresh strength to our people."

Franklin D. Roosevelt

## How will you change the world today?

## What good happened today?

## Who or what is inspiring you?

One of the biggest obstacles to making a start on climate change is that it has become a cliché before it has even been understood."

Tim Flannery

# How will you change the world today?

## What good happened today?

_____
_____
_____
_____
_____
_____
_____

## Who or what is inspiring you?

_____
_____
_____
_____
_____
_____
_____

"If you don't act against climate change, then no matter how much money you leave for your children, it'll not even cover their healthcare bills, due to living in an unhealthy planet."

Abhijit Naskar

# How will you change the world today?

## What good happened today?

## Who or what is inspiring you?

"Anybody who doesn't see the impact of climate change is really, and I would say, myopic. They don't see the reality. It's so evident that we are destroying Mother Earth."

Juan Manuel Santos

# How will you change the world today?

## What good happened today?

## Who or what is inspiring you?

"Climate change isn't an 'issue' to add to the list of things to worry about, next to health care and taxes. It is a civilizational wake-up call."

Naomi Klein

# How will you change the world today?

## What good happened today?

## Who or what is inspiring you?

"Climate change is the environmental challenge of this generation, and it is imperative that we act before it's too late."

John Delaney

# How will you change the world today?

## What good happened today?

## Who or what is inspiring you?

> "First life, then spaces, then buildings —
> the other way around never works."
>
> Jan Gehl

# How will you change the world today?

## What good happened today?

## Who or what is inspiring you?

"At present, we are stealing the future, selling it in the present, and calling it gross domestic product."

Paul Hawken

# How will you change the world today?

## What good happened today?

## Who or what is inspiring you?

"Be the change you want to see in this world."

Mahatma Gandhi

# How will you change the world today?

## What good happened today?

## Who or what is inspiring you?

If you enjoyed using this journal, consider reading the companion book, "Sustainability for the Rest of Us: Your No-Bullshit, Five-Point Plan for Saving the Planet."

Also, please take the time to show this journal some love on social media, your favorite online retailer or bookstore, and by spreading the word to family, friends, and especially those who we need to bring onside in our fight for a better tomorrow.

Thank you.

www.ingramcontent.com/pod-product-compliance
Lightning Source LLC
Chambersburg PA
CBHW020328010526
44107CB00054B/2015